Alfred's Instrumental Easy Play-Along

Easy Christmas
Instrumental Solos

CONTENTS

Arranged by Bill Galliford, Ethan Neuburg and Tod Edmondson

ISBN-10: 0-7390-6219-0
ISBN-13: 978-0-7390-6219-7

Alfred

Track 2: Demo
Track 3: Play Along

BELIEVE
(from *The Polar Express*)

Words and Music by
ALAN SILVESTRI
and GLENN BALLARD

Moderately slow (♩ = 80)

33271

DECK THE HALL

Track 4: Demo
Track 5: Play Along

Traditional

DANCE OF THE SUGAR-PLUM FAIRY

(from *The Nutcracker Suite*)

Track 6: Demo
Track 7: Play Along

By PETER ILYICH TCHAIKOVSKY

Moderately slow (♩ = 112)

Track 8: Demo
Track 9: Play Along

THE FIRST NOËL

Traditional

Moderately ♩ = 92

FELIZ NAVIDAD

Words and Music by
JOSÉ FELICIANO

FROSTY THE SNOWMAN

Track 12: Demo
Track 13: Play Along

Words and Music by
STEVE NELSON and JACK ROLLINS

33271

HARK! THE HERALD ANGELS SING

Track 14: Demo
Track 15: Play Along

Music by
FELIX MENDELSSOHN

JINGLE BELL ROCK

Words and Music by
JOE BEAL and JIM BOOTHE

33271

JINGLE BELLS

By J. PIERPONT

Moderately fast (♩ = 144)
(♩ = 72 This represents the song pulse feel counted in two.)

LET IT SNOW! LET IT SNOW! LET IT SNOW!

Track 20: Demo
Track 21: Play Along

Music by
JULE STYNE

THE LITTLE DRUMMER BOY

Track 22: Demo
Track 23: Play Along

Words and Music by
HARRY SIMEONE, HENRY ONORATI
and KATHERINE DAVIS

Moderately (♩ = 138)
(♩ = 69 This represents the song pulse feel counted in two.)

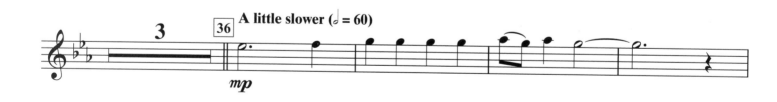

A little slower (♩ = 60)

SILENT NIGHT

Track 24: Demo
Track 25: Play Along

Words and Music by
JOSEPH MOHR and FRANZ GRUBER

Track 26: Demo
Track 27: Play Along

SLEIGH RIDE

By LEROY ANDERSON

Moderately bright, with spirit (♩ = 184)
(♩ = 92 This represents the song pulse feel counted in two.)

YOU'RE A MEAN ONE, MR. GRINCH
(from Dr. Seuss' *How The Grinch Stole Christmas*)

Track 28: Demo
Track 29: Play Along

Music by
ALBERT HAGUE

33271

PARTS OF A FLUTE AND FINGERING CHART

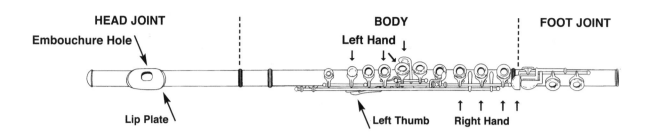

HEAD JOINT
Embouchure Hole
Lip Plate

BODY
Left Hand
Left Thumb
Right Hand

FOOT JOINT

● = press the key.
○ = do not press the key.

When there are two fingerings given for a note, use the first one unless the alternate fingering is suggested.

When two enharmonic notes are given together (F♯ and G♭ as an example), they sound the same pitch and are played the same way.